# tick, tick . . . BOOM!

# tick, tick . . . BOOM!

**The Complete Book and Lyrics**

*Book, Music, and Lyrics*
by Jonathan Larson

*Script Consultant*
David Auburn

**APPLAUSE**
**THEATRE & CINEMA BOOKS**

Published in 2009 by Applause Theatre & Cinema Books
An Imprint of Globe Pequot
4501 Forbes Boulevard, Suite 200
Lanham, Maryland 20706

All photographs of the Off-Broadway production are by Joan Marcus.
The photograph of Neil Patrick Harris appears courtesy of Menier Chocolate Factory.

Distributed by NATIONAL BOOK NETWORK

Book design by Lesley Kunikis

Library of Congress Cataloging-in-Publication Data is available upon request.

ISBN 978-1-55783-744-8

www.applausepub.com

# Contents

## Introduction

**by Robyn Goodman**

In 1990, when I was running Second Stage Theatre with Carole Rothman, I met a lanky and self-assured young composer/lyricist named Jonathan Larson. He told me that he would change musical theatre forever by introducing rock and roll into its vocabulary. I had just finished listening to a rock monologue he was composing about turning thirty in 1990, and, although this statement seemed a bit grandiose, I was impressed with his talent. His music was thrilling, and he had captured something about life that was both original and universal . . . pursuing one's dreams at all costs. And he had done it with passion and humor.

In September 1990, the Second Stage, in conjunction with Jon's best friend Victoria Leacock, produced a workshop of Jon's monologue *Boho Days*. The show had brilliance, but the story was convoluted. We begged Jon to work on structure and let an actor play the part in a full production. He refused, but he and I stayed in touch. In fact, he even told me that he had this crazy idea for a rock-and-roll version of *La Boheme* and sent me the first three amazing songs. I took him to City Opera to see a production, and through the entire opera he whispered to me how he was updating the story to the world of the '90s and all his struggling friends. He thought he would call it *Rent*. I smiled supportively. A year later, I left the theatre to produce television and missed the opportunity to produce, inarguably, the most important musical of my generation. And then the tragedy occurred. We lost Jonathan before *Rent* even opened.

Cut to the year 2000. I was just opening my own production office when Victoria, with the Larson family's permission, asked if I would like to join her in producing *Boho Days* Off-Broadway. She told me that since we'd produced it, there were three titles, five versions of the script, and many tapes of Jon singing versions of the songs. How could I resist? I suggested that my friend David Auburn, who had just received the Pulitzer Prize for the play *Proof*, look over the material with the young director Scott Schwartz and see what they could make of it. Victoria and I were thrilled when they came back with a structure that included three characters—Jon, his girlfriend, and his best friend. They framed it around his birthday party and the crisis many artists face when balancing paying the bills with pursuing their craft. They energized the dramatic structure with mostly Jon's own words and, with the Larson family's permission, only added one song from *Supurbia* (Jon's unproduced musical) called "Come to Your Senses." We made two extraordinary additions to the team: Stephen Oremus came aboard to orchestrate the music and Christopher Gatelli to do the musical staging. We booked the Jane Street Theatre in the West Village for its rock club atmosphere and planned to open on June 14, 2001.

The search for the perfect actor to play Jon was spearheaded by David Caperelliotis, who from the very beginning urged us to see a young actor named Raúl Esparza. Raúl had recently arrived from Chicago, where he had played mostly non-singing dramatic roles. We flipped over his audition and begged him to leave the show in which he was currently performing and join us. It would be his first leading part on the New York stage and we knew he would draw attention. He was then joined by the lovely Amy Spanger and ever-smooth Jerry Dixon. The addition of designers Anna Louizos, Ken Posner, David Zinn, and Jon Weston was the crowning touch. I can't imagine what angel was sitting on our shoulders; they were all so wonderful.

On second thought, of course I can. The angel was Jonathan Larson, and every night when Raúl would lift his eyes to the heavens at the end of the show, I knew he was with us. And yes, Jon, forgive me for doubting it even for a moment, you *have* changed the musical theatre forever. You welcomed in the next generation of composers who now grace our Broadway stages with exuberant new voices.

## Production Note

**tick, tick . . . BOOM!**
Book, Music, and Lyrics by Jonathan Larson
Directed by Scott Schwartz

*tick, tick . . . BOOM!* was originally produced at the Jane Street Theatre by Victoria Leacock, Robyn Goodman, Dede Harris, Lorie Coen Levy, and Beth Smith. It opened on June 13, 2001.

# Cast and Credits

## Original Off-Broadway Performance

**Cast**

JON
Raúl Esparza

SUSAN
Amy Spanger

MICHAEL
Jerry Dixon

**Set Design**
Anna Louizos

**Sound Design**
Jon Wetson

**Costume Design**
David Zinn

**Lighting Design**
Kenneth Posner

**Hair Design**
Antonio Soddu

**Musical Staging**
Christopher Gattelli

**Casting**
David Caparelliotis

**Press Agent**
Richard Kornberg & Associates

**Production Stage Manager**
Ed Fitzgerald

**Production Manager**
Kai Brothers

**General Manager**
Roy Gabay

**Associate Producers**
Ruth and Stephen Hendel, Stephen Semlitz and Cathy Glaser

**Script Consultant**
David Auburn

**Music Supervisor/Orchestrator/Arranger**
Stephen Oremus

**Keyboard**
Stephen Oremus

**Guitar**
Matt Beck

**Bass**
Konrad Adderley

**Drums**
Clayton Craddock

## Musical Numbers

1. 30/90
2. Green Green Dress
3. Johnny Can't Decide
4. Sunday
5. No More
6. Therapy
7. Real Life
8. Sugar
9. See Her Smile
10. Come to Your Senses
11. Why
12. 30/90 Reprise
13. Louder Than Words

*Spoken lines are indicated in upper- and lowercase.*

# tick, tick . . . BOOM!

## Characters

**JON**, twenty-nine

**MICHAEL**, thirty

**SUSAN**, late twenties

Other characters to be played by the actors playing Michael and Susan.

# Scene 1

[*In black.*]

**TICK . . . TICK . . . TICK . . . TICK . . . TICK . . . TICK . . .**

**JON**

The sound you are hearing is not a technical problem. It is not a musical cue. It is not a joke. It is the sound of one man's mounting anxiety. I . . . am that man.

[*Lights up.*]

Hi. I'm Jon, and lately I keep hearing that sound, that ticking. It's not a big deal. It's actually kind of pleasant, like a watch.

In one week I'll be thirty. Three-zero. Older than my dad was when I was born. Older than Napoleon was when he . . . did something that was probably extremely impressive at the time—I'm not a historian. I'm a composer. Sorry, a "promising young composer." I should have kids of my own by now, a career, but instead I've been "promising" for so long I'm afraid I'm starting to break the fucking promise.

And I want to get some writing done, but I keep hearing those tick-ticks. And sometimes, after a couple of them, I'll hear something else—a distant BOOM, like a bomb has gone off not too far away and the next one might be closer and I'd better look out.

**TICK . . . TICK . . . BOOM!**

[HE *bangs a crash on the piano.*]

So that's where we are. It's a Saturday night in January 1990 in my apartment on the edge of SoHo. I'm trying to work, trying to enjoy what remains of my extremely late twenties, and trying to ignore the tick-tick-booms.

## 1. 30/90

STOP THE CLOCK—TAKE TIME OUT
TIME TO REGROUP BEFORE YOU LOSE THE BOUT
FREEZE THE FRAME—BACK IT UP
TIME TO REFOCUS BEFORE THEY WRAP IT UP

YEARS ARE GETTING SHORTER
LINES ON YOUR FACE ARE GETTING LONGER
FEEL LIKE YOU'RE TREADING WATER
BUT THE RIP TIDE'S GETTING STRONGER
DON'T PANIC—DON'T JUMP SHIP
CAN'T FIGHT IT—LIKE TAXES
AT LEAST IT HAPPENS ONLY ONCE IN YOUR LIFE

THEY'RE SINGING HAPPY BIRTHDAY
YOU JUST WANT TO LAY DOWN AND CRY
NOT JUST ANOTHER BIRTHDAY
IT'S THIRTY NINETY

WHY CAN'T YOU STAY TWENTY-NINE, HELL
YOU STILL FEEL LIKE YOU'RE TWENTY-TWO
TURN THIRTY 1990—BANG, YOU'RE DEAD
WHAT CAN YOU DO?
WHAT CAN YOU DO?
WHAT CAN YOU DO?

Hey, you know what? Forget it. It's no big deal. What's thirty? Just, you know, the end of youth.

**MICHAEL**

Jon, you've got to chill.

**JON**

Michael. My roommate, my oldest and dearest friend. We grew up together, moved to Manhattan, and were starving artists together. Were. Mike was a terrific actor, but he gave it up to become a big-time market research exec. Now, he's the proud owner of a brand-new BMW. Mike, you're thirty. Are you happy?

**MICHAEL**

Thirty's great. Thirty's like Newark Airport.

**JON**

Newark Airport?

**MICHAEL**

Hard to get to, but once you're here, fewer delays.

**JON**

Mike spends way too much time traveling on business.

**MICHAEL**

CLEAR THE RUNWAY—MAKE ANOTHER PASS
TRY ONE MORE APPROACH
BEFORE YOU'RE OUT OF GAS

**JON**

FRIENDS ARE GETTING FATTER
HAIRS ON YOUR HEAD ARE GETTING THINNER
FEEL LIKE A CLEANUP BATTER
ON A TEAM THAT AIN'T A WINNER?

**MICHAEL**

DON'T FREAK OUT—DON'T STRIKE OUT
CAN'T FIGHT IT—LIKE CITY HALL

**JON**

AT LEAST YOU'RE NOT ALONE
YOUR FRIENDS ARE THERE TOO—
THEY'RE SINGING HAPPY BIRTHDAY

**JON and MICHAEL**

YOU JUST WISH YOU COULD RUN AWAY

**JON**

WHO CARES ABOUT A BIRTHDAY?—BUT

**JON and MICHAEL**

THIRTY NINETY—HEY!

**JON**

CAN YOU BE OPTIMISTIC

**JON and MICHAEL**

YOU'RE NO LONGER THE INGENUE
TURN THIRTY 1990

**JON**

BOOM—YOU'RE PASSÉ

**JON and MICHAEL**

WHAT CAN YOU DO?

| JON | MICHAEL |
|---|---|
| WHAT CAN YOU DO? | OOH |
| WHAT CAN YOU DO? | |

**SUSAN**

Jon, breathe.

**JON**

Susan's here too, My girlfriend. We've been together two years, it's great, she's great, she's a dancer, but supports herself teaching ballet to wealthy and untalented children. She starts talking about the birthday party she's planning for next week.

**SUSAN**

You're gonna enjoy it, I promise. I sent out the invitations, the apartment will be full of friends, we'll have a great time.

**JON**

She's right. Goddamn it, I am looking forward to it!

**SUSAN**

And you'll play "Happy Birthday," we'll all sing . . .

**JON**

I have to play it?

**SUSAN**

Sure.

**JON**

I can't play "Happy Birthday" for myself.

**SUSAN**

Why not?

**JON**

I've forgotten it.

I realize I've forgotten how to play the piano completely. Holy shit, have I forgotten how to play the piano because I don't want to play "Happy Birthday" because I don't want to—Oh God—grow up?

| **JON** | **MICHAEL and SUSAN** |
| --- | --- |
| PETER PAN AND TINKER-BELL | AH . . . |
| WHICH WAY TO NEVER- | |
| NEVERLAND? | |
| EMERALD CITY'S GONE TO HELL | |
| SINCE THE WIZARD | |

**ALL**

BLEW OFF HIS COMMAND

**JON**

ON THE STREET YOU HEAR THE VOICES—
LOST CHILDREN, CROCODILES
YOU'RE NOT INTO
MAKING CHOICES, WICKED WITCHES,
POPPY FIELDS OR MEN BEHIND THE CURTAIN
TIGER LILIES, RUBY SLIPPERS

**ALL**

CLOCK IS TICKING—THAT'S FOR CERTAIN

| **JON** | **MICHAEL and SUSAN** |
|---|---|
| THEY'RE SINGING HAPPY BIRTHDAY | HAPPY BIRTHDAY |
| I JUST WISH IT ALL WERE A DREAM | |
| IT FEELS MUCH MORE LIKE DOOMSDAY | |
| FUCK | |

**ALL**

THIRTY NINETY—

| **JON** | **MICHAEL and SUSAN** |
|---|---|
| SEEMS LIKE I'M IN FOR A TWISTER | AH . . . |
| I DON'T SEE A RAINBOW— | |
| DO YOU? | |

**ALL**

TURN THIRTY IN THE NINETIES

| **JON** | **MICHAEL and SUSAN** |
|---|---|
| INTO MY HANDS NOW— | |
| THE BALL IS PASSED | |
| I WANT THE SPOILS— | AH . . . |
| BUT NOT TOO FAST | AH . . . |
| WORLD IS CALLING— | |
| IT'S NOW OR NEVERLAND | AH . . . |
| WHY CAN'T I STAY A CHILD | THIRTY NINETY |

| **JON** | **MICHAEL and SUSAN** |
| --- | --- |
| FOREVER | |
| AND THIRTY NINETY THIRTY | THIRTY NINETY |
| NINETY | |
| THIRTY NINETY THIRTY | |
| NINETY | |
| THIRTY NINETY | |

**ALL**

THIRTY THIRTY NINETY
WHAT CAN I DO—?

**MICHAEL and SUSAN**

THIRTY NINETY
THIRTY THIRTY NINETY, OOH

ALL
WHAT CAN I DO?

# Scene 2

**MICHAEL**

Hey, tomorrow night I want to show you the new place.

**JON**

Oh yeah. Michael's moving out. He's making so much money he bought an apartment with the bathtub in the bathroom.

**TICK . . . TICK . . . TICK**

**MICHAEL**

And will you please let me set up an interview with my firm?

**JON**

Lately Mike's been worried my musical theatre career isn't going anywhere. And I'm not sure I blame him.

**MICHAEL**

You'll love it. You'll be promoted faster than I was.

**JON**

I haven't decided, Mike. I'm still enjoying my pre-midlife crisis.

**MICHAEL**

At least think it over.

**JON**

I'll think it over.

**MICHAEL**

All I'm asking. See you in the morning.

**JON**

You going to bed? It's early.

**MICHAEL**

I'm still on London time. 'Night.

**SUSAN**

'Night.

**JON**

Sleep well.

[MIKE *exits.*]

I need some air. I grab a joint and escape to the roof. It's cold. I hear a few tick-booms. I've spent the last five years writing a musical called *Superbia*, and we're doing a workshop this week. It's the other reason I'm freaking out. We're putting the show on its feet before an audience for the first time. I'm all hope and apprehension. It's the best thing I've ever done, and if the workshop goes well, and if I can get my so-called agent, Rosa Stevens, who hasn't returned my calls in over six months, to actually come and see it, the show might get some buzz. And if there's enough buzz, the show might be produced, and if the show is produced, it might be a hit—and if it is, I won't have to take the marketing job and I can buy the BMW anyway, and I will have done it all before I'm thirty, or at least I can fudge the dates to make it sound that way in my Sunday *Times* Arts & Leisure profile.

I am not proud of this line of thinking.

But it's not my fault! It's hard for people born after 1960 to be idealistic or original. We know what happens to ideals. They're assassinated or corrupted or co-opted. It's 1990 for God's sake. It is not an exciting period. It is not a period of ferment. It's fucking stodgy is what it is—conservative, complacent, obtuse, and unimaginative. Or, to put it another way: George Bush is president of the United States.

After a minute, Susan comes up from downstairs. She's wearing the dress we had made—a friend who works at the diner with me designed it. Everyone we know wants to do something else.

**SUSAN**

What do you think?

**JON**

[*Smoking a joint.*]

Looks good.

**SUSAN**

Are you okay?

**JON**

Sure. Just like the view. The river . . .

**SUSAN**

Are you really thinking about going to work with Mike?

**JON**

I've been waiting tables for four years, Suze. I always thought by the time I was thirty I'd either have a hit show or a really lucrative sell-out career, but I've got neither. Jesus. Has turning thirty always sucked? Or is our generation different because we've never grown up? Never had a real test. A depression. A world war, Vietnam—maybe that's what I need.

**SUSAN**

Good idea. I'll try to arrange that for you.

**JON**

Yeah? Thanks.

**SUSAN**

Anytime, honey.

**JON**

Susan takes my hand, warming up the whole roof. We look out over the river. The lights from the prison barge flicker in her eyes.

You really look beautiful.

**SUSAN**

Thanks.

**JON**

That dress looks incredible on you.

## 2. Green Green Dress

DEEP DARK VELVET
HUGS YOUR SILHOUETTE
BLACK SILK STOCKINGS
YOU'RE MY JULIET

SOFT BLOND HAIR, BABY
BABY BLUE EYES

COOL ME DOWN
BEFORE I JUMP INTO YOUR THIGHS

THE GREEN GREEN DRESS
TWENTY BUTTONS AND A STRAP
THE GREEN GREEN DRESS
WHAT A PLEASURE TO UNWRAP

GREEN GREEN DRESS
OH, WHAT IT CAN DO
OH, WHAT THE GREEN GREEN DRESS
DOES TO ME—ON YOU
ME—ON YOU

**SUSAN**

LET'S FIND A CHAIR
WHERE WE CAN SIT AND TALK
OR GET SOME FRESH AIR
MAYBE WE CAN TAKE A WALK

TELL ME WHAT YOU'RE THINKING
TALK ABOUT YOUR DAY
TELL ME WHAT TO DO
I'LL DO ANYTHING YOU SAY

**BOTH**

THE GREEN GREEN DRESS
TWENTY BUTTONS AND A STRAP
THE GREEN GREEN DRESS

**JON**

WHAT A PLEASURE TO UNWRAP

**BOTH**

GREEN DRESS
OH, WHAT IT CAN DO
OH, WHAT THE GREEN GREEN DRESS

| JON | SUSAN |
| --- | --- |
| DOES TO ME—ON YOU | OOOH |
| ME—ON YOU | YOU |

**SUSAN**

CAN I HEAR YOU LAUGH, BABE?
CAN YOU MAKE ME SMILE?
I'LL FORGET WHAT'S ON MY MIND
FOR A WHILE

**JON**

CAN I TIE YOU UP, LOVE
IF YOU TELL ME YES
I'LL UNBUTTON EVERY BUTTON
DOWN YOUR GREEN GREEN DRESS—OW!

**BOTH**

THE GREEN GREEN DRESS
TWENTY BUTTONS AND A STRAP
THE GREEN GREEN DRESS
WHAT A PLEASURE TO UNWRAP

GREEN DRESS
OH, WHAT IT CAN DO
OH, WHAT THE GREEN GREEN DRESS

| JON | SUSAN |
| --- | --- |
| DOES TO ME—ON YOU | OOOH |
| ME—ON YOU | YOU |

**BOTH**

THE GREEN GREEN DRESS
ME—ON YOU

**JON**

THE GREEN GREEN DRESS

**SUSAN**

THE GREEN GREEN DRESS

**JON**

THE GREEN GREEN DRESS

**SUSAN**

THE GREEN GREEN DRESS

**BOTH**

THE GREEN GREEN DRESS

# Scene 3

**JON**

6 a.m. The sky glows. Somewhere a bird chirps. I want to shoot it.

**SUSAN**

Go back to sleep.

**JON**

I can't. I'm too wired. Sorry I woke you. I'll just—

**SUSAN**

No, stay, it's okay.

[*Beat.*]

Jon, you know what?

**JON**

What?

**SUSAN**

We could just get out of here.

**JON**

What do you mean?

**SUSAN**

Live somewhere else. Somewhere beautiful, near a beach . . . Cape Cod . . .

**JON**

Leave New York?

**SUSAN**

Why not? I think the city just wears you down. Every time I cross the Triboro I feel five years older.

**JON**

If I want to write shows, I have to be here. If you want to be a dancer—

**SUSAN**

I am a dancer. I'd still be a dancer if I lived in New England, but I'd have a dishwasher.

[*Beat.*]

At least think it over? For me?

**JON**

Ah. More to think over.

## 3. Johnny Can't Decide

BREAK OF DAY—THE DAWN IS HERE
JOHNNY'S UP AND PACING
COMPROMISE OR PERSEVERE?
HIS MIND IS RACING
JOHNNY HAS NO GUIDE—JOHNNY WANTS TO HIDE
CAN HE MAKE A MARK—IF HE GIVES UP HIS SPARK?
JOHNNY CAN'T DECIDE

**SUSAN**

SUSAN LONGS TO LIVE BY THE SEA
SHE'S THROUGH WITH COMPETITION
SUSAN WANTS A FAMILY
JOHNNY'S GOT A TOUGH DECISION
JOHNNY HAS NO GUIDE

**SUSAN and JON**

JOHNNY WANTS TO HIDE
CAN HE SETTLE DOWN—AND STILL NOT DROWN?
JOHNNY CAN'T DECIDE

**MICHAEL**

MICHAEL'S GONNA HAVE IT ALL
HIS LUCK WILL NEVER END
JOHNNY'S BACKED AGAINST THE WALL
CAN HE BEND HIS DREAMS JUST LIKE HIS FRIEND?

**JON**

JOHNNY SEES THAT

**JON and SUSAN**

SUSAN'S RIGHT

**ALL**

AMBITION EATS RIGHT THROUGH YOU
MICHAEL DOESN'T SEE WHY JOHNNY HOLDS ON TIGHT
TO THE THINGS THAT JOHNNY FEELS ARE TRUE
JOHNNY HAS NO GUIDE—JOHNNY WANTS TO HIDE
HOW CAN YOU SOAR—IF YOU'RE NAILED TO THE FLOOR?
JOHNNY CAN'T DECIDE

**JON**

I want to write music. I want to sit down right now at my piano and write a song that people will listen to and remember, and do the same thing every morning for the rest of my life.

**ALL**

JOHNNY HAS NO GUIDE—JOHNNY WANTS TO HIDE
HOW DO YOU KNOW WHEN IT'S TIME TO LET GO?

**JON**

JOHNNY CAN'T DECIDE
JOHNNY CAN'T DECIDE
JOHNNY CAN'T DECIDE
JOHNNY CAN'T DECIDE
DECIDE DECIDE, DECIDE
DECIDE
JOHNNY CAN'T DECIDE

**MICHAEL and SUSAN**

JOHNNY CAN'T DECIDE
DECIDE
JOHNNY CAN'T DECIDE
DECIDE
DECIDE DECIDE, DECIDE
OOH

**JON**

But right now I have to go to work.

# Scene 4

[*SFX of diner.*]

**#1 [MICHAEL]**

Straight back and to your left.

**#2 [SUSAN]**

Pick up those fucking eggs!

**#1**

[Brrring-Bbbbrrrrring.]

**#2**

We're out of milk!

**#1**

Who took my rye bread?

**#2**

Four waters to table seven!

**#1**

I'm sorry, we don't deliver on Sunday—I need table three for two, yesterday—

**#2**

Is there a list?

**#1**

Harrington! Harrington??

**#2**

Kaplan—K-a-p-l-a-n—for seven.

**JON**

ORDER!

**#1**

No—I'm sorry—those people were here first. We don't have tables for seven.

**#2**

Are we in Smoking?

**JON**

TENSION!

**#1**

I'll have the salad Nick-oyz and some holly bread.

**JON**

BALANCE!

**#2**

I SAID I wanted an omelet with no yolks! That's why you're just a waiter!

**JON**

Brunch.

## 4. Sunday

SUNDAY
IN THE BLUE
SILVER CHROMIUM DINER
ON THE GREEN
PURPLE YELLOW RED STOOLS
SIT THE FOOLS
WHO SHOULD EAT AT HOME
INSTEAD THEY PAY ON

**ALL**

SUNDAY

**JON**

FOR A COOL
ORANGE JUICE OR A BAGEL
ON THE SOFT
GREEN CYLINDRICAL STOOLS
SIT THE FOOLS
DRINKING CINNAMON COFFEE
OR DECAFFINATED TEA

**ALL**

FOREVER
IN THE BLUE
SILVER CHROMIUM DINER

**JON**

DRIPS THE GREEN
ORANGE VIOLET DROOL

**ALL**

FROM THE FOOLS

**JON**

WHO'D PAY LESS AT HOME
DRINKING COFFEE

**ALL**

LIGHT
AND DARK

**JON**

AND CHOLESTEROL
AND BUMS, BUMS, BUMS,
BUMS, BUMS, BUMS, BUMS, BUMS, BUMS,

**ALL**

PEOPLE SCREAMING FOR THEIR TOAST
IN A SMALL SOHO CAFE

**JON**

ON AN ISLAND IN

**ALL**

TWO RIVERS
ON AN ORDINARY
SUNDAY
SUNDAY
SUNDAY

**JON**

BRUNCH

# Scene 5

**JON**

I sink into a soft leather seat. Michael guns twelve fuel-injected Bavarian-engineered market-research-funded cylinders across Houston Street.

His new Beemer . . . is fucking awesome. The stereo. The sleekness . . .

**MICHAEL**

Check out the seat.

**JON**

The seat? . . . The seat is HEATED.

**MICHAEL**

And you can adjust it.

**JON**

This is a car that allows you to adjust the temperature of your ass.

Michael picked me up from the diner so we can check out his new apartment. We zhhhooooom—past the inhabitants of SoHo, wearing black, black, black, black . . .

**JON**

Past the East Village kids with purple pink green blue spike-buzz cuts, jutting through deconstructed SILENCE = DEATH T-shirts . . .

Past the Windex, the squeegees, the outstretched palms, the Bowery Night Train philosophers. How can I possibly leave this behind?

In a flash, we're rolling into a circular driveway with a marble fountain in the center.

He tosses the keys to the parking attendant as we breeze in through the smoked-glass revolving doors. Stainless-steel kitchen. Polyurethaned wood floors. View of the 59th Street Bridge. It's still being remodeled—Remodeled! But my God . . .

**MICHAEL**

Jon, welcome to Victory Towers.

## 5. No More

NO MORE—
WALKING UP SIX FLIGHTS OF STAIRS
OR THROWING DOWN THE KEY BECAUSE THERE IS NO BUZZER

NO MORE—
WALKING THIRTEEN BLOCKS WITH THIRTY POUNDS
OF LAUNDRY IN THE FUCKING DEAD OF WINTER

NO MORE—FAULTY WIRING
NO MORE—PAINTED FLOORS
NO MORE SPITTING OUT MY ULTRA BRITE
ON TOP OF DIRTY DISHES IN THE ONE AND ONLY SINK
HELLO TO MY WALK-IN CLOSETS
TIDY AS PARK AVENUE
HELLO, MY BUTCHER BLOCK TABLE

I COULD GET USED—I COULD GET USED

**JON**

Hello? [HE *checks out the echo in the walk-in closet.*]

**MICHAEL**

I COULD GET USED TO YOU

NO MORE—

CLIMBING OVER SLEEPING PEOPLE
BEFORE YOU GET OUT THE DOOR OF YOUR OWN BUILDING

**BOTH**

NO MORE—

**MICHAEL**

NOXIOUS FUMES—FROM GAS HEATERS THAT ARE ILLEGAL

**JON**

OR WILL BLOW UP WHILE YOU ARE SLEEPING

**MICHAEL**

NO MORE—

**JON**

LEAKY CEILINGS

**MICHAEL**

NO MORE—

**JON**

HOLES IN THE FLOOR

**BOTH**

NO MORE

**JON**

TAKING A SHOWER IN THE KITCHEN
WHILE YOUR ROOMMATE'S EATING BREAKFAST

**BOTH**

AND YOU'RE GETTING WATER ON HIS CORNFLAKES

HELLO TO SHINY NEW PARQUET WOOD FLOORS
AS WAXED AS A WEALTHY GIRL'S LEGS
HELLO, DEAR MR. DISHWASHER

| **MICHAEL** | **JON** |
| --- | --- |
| I COULD GET USED | I COULD GET USED |
| I COULD GET USED | I COULD GET USED |
| I COULD GET USED TO YOU | TO YOU |

**BOTH**

NO MORE—

**JON**

EXOTIC

**BOTH**

NO MORE—

**MICHAEL**

NEUROTIC

**BOTH**

NO MORE—ANYTHING BUT PLEASANTLY ROBOTIC

| **MICHAEL** | **JON** |
|---|---|
| WE'RE MOVIN ON UP<br>TO THE EAST SIDE | WE'RE MOVIN ON UP<br>TO THE EAST SIDE |

**BOTH**

TO A DELUXE APARTMENT IN THE SKY—

[*Dance break.*]

HELLO TO DEAR MR. DOORMAN
WHO LOOKS LIKE CAPTAIN KANGAROO
HELLO, DEAR FELLOW—AND HOW DO YOU DO?

| **MICHAEL** | **JON** |
|---|---|
| I COULD GET USED<br>EVEN SEDUCED | I COULD GET USED<br>EVEN SEDUCED |

**BOTH**

I COULD GET USED TO YOU!

# Scene 6

**MICHAEL**

What do you think?

**JON**

Back home in SoHo, Michael is trying on one of three new Gucci belts he's just bought.

**MICHAEL**

Well?

**JON**

I don't know, Mike. I haven't owned three belts over the course of my entire life.

**MICHAEL**

Try it. It's a good feeling.

**JON**

I feel relaxed, just hanging out with Mike on a Sunday night.

Mike and I met at Camp Shawanga, eight years old. During the first week, Mike was thick with Dion Cappporimo, the kid who set fires in the outhouse and bombed the girls with M-80s. I hung with Jim Shanahan, volleyball team captain and every counselor's favorite camper. By week two, Mike and I had dumped our old new best friends and found each other. We ended up at the same high school, acting in shows together, best friends through it all.

**MICHAEL**

How's Susan?

**JON**

Okay.

**MICHAEL**

Just okay?

**JON**

She wants us to move to Cape Cod.

**MICHAEL**

I am so sorry.

**JON**

No, maybe I should really think about it.

**MICHAEL**

You're not a Cape Cod guy. Listen. I've got a better idea. I want you to come to the office tomorrow.

**JON**

Oh no.

**MICHAEL**

They're doing a brainstorming session for a new product. Real creative stuff. You'd be perfect for it. I told them all about you. Please? Just come in, no commitment, I promise. Just get your feet wet?

**JON**

Oh, what the hell. Sure, I'll do it.

**MICHAEL**

Excellent. You won't be sorry. I'm gonna go pack.

**JON**

You going away again?

**MICHAEL**

Tomorrow night. Meeting in Atlanta. Departing Newark 6 p.m. Drive me?

**JON**

Sure. Is David busy?

**MICHAEL**

I can't ask David right now.

**JON**

Why not?

**MICHAEL**

It's . . . complicated. We . . .

[*The phone.*]

**JON**

Whoops. Sorry, Mike. Hello?

**DAD**

HEL-lo.

**JON**

Hi, Dad.

My weekly call from White Plains.

**DAD**

How's it feel to be an old man?

**JON**

I'm not thirty yet, Dad.

**DAD**

Make good dough at brunch?

**JON**

Not bad.

**DAD**

Your sister just got a $40,000 bonus from the law firm. And of course you heard the news about Chuck.

**JON**

My brother-in-law.

**DAD**

Sold another screenplay! The one he's been working on for a month.

**JON**

Arrrgggh.

**DAD**

Isn't that marvelous?

**JON**

[*Call-waiting beep.*]

Hold on, Dad. I'm getting another call.

**ROSA [SUSAN]**

Jonathan? It's Rosa.

**JON**

Rosa? My God, it's Rosa Stevens, my agent! That bitch. She hasn't returned my calls for months. Why is she calling now, on a Sunday night? Is she cutting me loose?

**ROSA**

Are you excited?

**JON**

What?

**ROSA**

Are you excited about your workshop next week?

**JON**

She remembered the workshop!

**ROSA**

I made a few calls, we ought to have some interesting people there for you to meet.

**JON**

She made a few calls!

**ROSA**

I just wanted to say good luck, honey. See you soon.

**JON**

Good luck! Interesting people! Rosa, what an angel, she's a sweetheart, I love that woman, she—whoops. Sorry, Dad.

**DAD**

No problem. That's all the news anyway. Talk to you soon.

**JON**

Dad signs off the conversation, as always, with the old Bob and Ray line:

**DAD**

Write if you get work.

**JON**

And I reply, as always, with "Hang by your thumbs."

**MOM [SUSAN]**

Oh, and Jonnie?

**JON**

My mother has been on the line the entire time.

**MOM**

You know you can always move in with us for a while,

[DAD *grunts.*]

if you need to.

[DAD *grunts.*]

**JON**

Thanks, Ma.

For the first time in months I think I might not need to. I'm just sitting down to do some writing when . . .

[*Phone ring.*]

**SUSAN**

Jon?

**JON**

Susan. Hey.

**SUSAN**

Hey.

**JON**

You want to come over?

**SUSAN**

I guess I was hoping you'd come up here.

**JON**

Susan lives in an illegal sublet on 96th and York.

It's pretty late.

**SUSAN**

Come over. We'll watch HBO.

**JON**

She has pirated cable.

I'm supposed to go into Michael's office tomorrow.

**SUSAN**

Sleep here, you'll be closer in the morning anyway.

[*Beat.*]

Jon. Are you weighing whether the trip up here is worth the cable TV?

**JON**

No!

**SUSAN**

You are, aren't you?

**JON**

Of course not.

**SUSAN**

I mean, I would be in the apartment too.

**JON**

And I'd be here. It's just as easy for you to come down to SoHo.

**SUSAN**

But it's late and it's New York and you're a guy, and I'm already in pajamas.

**JON**

Suze, it's two subways and a bus.

**SUSAN**

Take a cab.

**JON**

I can't afford cabs.

**SUSAN**

Well, God, forget it if it's that much trouble.

**JON**

No, it's, I just, I was planning on doing some work tonight.

**SUSAN**

You're going to write the great American musical in the next six hours?

**JON**

Hey, stop it. You know I've had trouble working. I could use some encouragement. I'm not trying to avoid a commute.

**SUSAN**

That's not what I'm saying.

**JON**

That's what you're inferring.

**SUSAN**

No, you mean that's what I'm implying. And I'm not implying it, you inferred it.

**JON**

Wait, what?

**SUSAN**

I can't believe we're fighting about this. If we're going to argue, let's argue about something important. Let's argue about moving up to New England, not about who's going to take the subway—

**JON**

Hold it, we're on New England now?

**SUSAN**

Should we not be?

**JON**

Why should we be?

**SUSAN**

Are you saying we can't talk?

**JON**

Are you saying we're NOT talking?

**SUSAN**

What are you saying?

**JON**

What are YOU saying? I'm saying—

## 6. Therapy

I FEEL BAD THAT
YOU FEEL BAD ABOUT
ME FEELING BAD ABOUT
YOU FEELING BAD ABOUT
WHAT I SAID ABOUT
WHAT YOU SAID ABOUT
ME NOT BEING ABLE TO SHARE A FEELING

**SUSAN**

IF I THOUGHT THAT
WHAT YOU THOUGHT WAS THAT
I HADN'T THOUGHT ABOUT
SHARING MY THOUGHTS THEN
MY REACTION TO

YOUR REACTION TO
MY REACTION
WOULD'VE BEEN MORE REVEALING

**JON**

I WAS AFRAID THAT
YOU'D BE AFRAID
IF I TOLD YOU
THAT I WAS AFRAID OF INTIMACY

IF YOU DON'T HAVE A PROBLEM
WITH MY PROBLEM
MAYBE THE PROBLEM'S
SIMPLY CODEPENDENCY

**SUSAN**

YES, I KNOW THAT
NOW YOU KNOW THAT
I DIDN'T KNOW THAT
YOU DIDN'T KNOW THAT WHEN
I SAID "NO" I MEANT
"YES, I KNOW" AND THAT
NOW I KNOW THAT YOU
KNEW THAT I KNEW YOU ADORED ME

**JON**

I WAS WRONG TO

**SUSAN**

SAY YOU WERE WRONG TO

**JON**

SAY I WAS WRONG ABOUT

**SUSAN**

YOU BEING WRONG

**JON**

WHEN YOU RANG TO SAY THAT

**SUSAN**

THE RING WAS THE WRONG THING TO BRING

**JON**

IF I MEANT WHAT I SAID
WHEN I SAID "RINGS BORED ME"

**BOTH**

I'M NOT MAD THAT
YOU GOT MAD WHEN
I GOT MAD WHEN YOU
SAID I SHOULD GO DROP DEAD

**JON**

IF I WERE YOU AND I'D
DONE WHAT I'D DONE I'D
DO WHAT YOU DID WHEN I
GAVE YOU THE RING HAVING
SAID WHAT I SAID

| **JON** | **SUSAN** |
|---|---|
| I FEEL BAD THAT | I |
| YOU FEEL BAD ABOUT | FEEL |
| ME FEELING BAD ABOUT | BADLY |
| YOU FEELING BAD ABOUT | ABOUT YOU |
| WHAT I SAID ABOUT | FEELING BADLY |
| WHAT YOU SAID ABOUT | ABOUT ME |
| ME NOT BEING ABLE TO | FEELING BADLY |
| SHARE A FEELING | ABOUT YOU |

I
THOUGHT
YOU
THOUGHT
I REACTED
SHALLOWLY
WHEN
I REACTED
TO YOU

I'M NOT MAD

YOU GOT MAD

GO DROP DEAD

IF I WERE YOU AND I'D
DONE WHAT I'D DONE I'D
DO WHAT YOU DID WHEN I
GAVE YOU THE RING HAVING
SAID WHAT I SAID

IF I THOUGHT THAT
WHAT YOU THOUGHT WAS
THAT
I HADN'T THOUGHT ABOUT
SHARING MY THOUGHTS
THEN
MY REACTION TO
YOUR REACTION TO
MY REACTION
WOULD'VE BEEN
MORE REVEALING

I'M NOT MAD THAT
YOU GOT MAD THAT
I GOT MAD WHEN YOU
SAID I SHOULD
GO DROP DEAD

IF I WERE YOU

BUT I'M NOT YOU

SAID WHAT YOU SAID

**JON**

BUT NOW IT'S OUT IN THE OPEN

**SUSAN**

NOW IT'S OFF OUR CHEST

**BOTH**

NOW IT'S FOUR A.M.
AND WE HAVE THERAPY TOMORROW,
IT'S TOO LATE TO SCREW
SO LET'S JUST GET SOME REST.

# Scene 7

**JON**

Monday morning. The walk to Michael's office takes me through Times Square. The Theater District. Jesus, look at these theaters. Every show's from London and every ticket costs a jaw-dropping fifty bucks. I guess that's what they want—the tourists, the snoring businessmen, the busloads of sweet old ladies from Connecticut with their 90-decibel cellophane-wrapped hard candies—I want no part of it.

But let's face it: Broadway is still the place. This is Parnassus for the musical theater world and for years I've been hiking in the foothills. Presenting songs in countless workshops, cutting demo tapes, scrounging for grants . . .

Once, at a seminar, on a day I will never forget, I got to have my work picked apart—and praised, a little—by my idol, a composer-lyricist so legendary his name may not be uttered aloud by me, Ste—— Sond——.

But I write musicals with rock music. A contradiction in terms. Broadway's about sixty years behind anything you hear on the radio. You can't put rock onstage—real rock, not warmed-over easy-listening pop, not plastic imitation '50s bubblegum. Nevertheless, that's what I'm trying to do with *Superbia*.

Could my show end up here? Is it good enough for Broadway, that magical street of dreams? Is it too good for Broadway, that shameless commercial whore? It's that raging mix of envy and contempt that's so . . . healthy.

# Scene 8

**JON**

Mike's office. Wow. Big cold lobby. Corporate America! Hundreds of people and they all look busy. Gray flannel execs.

**EXEC [MICHAEL]**

Tell the West Coast we need to liaise with corporate . . .

**JON**

Peacock-faced secretaries.

**SECRETARY [SUSAN]**

I'm sorry, he's in a meeting and can't possibly be reached.

**JON**

Temps in wrinkled khakis.

**TEMP [MICHAEL]**

Uh, I think the fax machine is jammed.

**JON**

And my favorite—the perfect women—the hard-driving, high-cheeked power haircut girls who cruise the avenues like sleek silver bullets.

**JUDY [SUSAN]**

Jonathan? Hi! Judy Wright. Michael's told me all about you. Come with me, I'll be leading the session. Help yourself to coffee . . .

**JON**

Tick . . . tick . . . tick . . .

**JUDY**

We are so glad you've come in! We love "creative" people. It's what we're all about!

**JON**

BOOM! BOOM! BOOM!

Conference room. Faux-wood-grain table. Aqua Naugahyde chairs.

**JUDY**

Everybody, this is Jonathan. He's going to help us out today. He writes musicals. You know, like Andrew Lloyd Weber.

[JON *grimaces.*]

Okay, let's get started! Today we're embarking on a major endeavor. We're developing a name for a breakthrough new product. A chemical to be used in cooking as a fat replacement! It's tasteless, has no calories, no fat, no cholesterol. In fact, it can't be absorbed into your digestive tract. This is going to give Americans a whole new kind of freedom in the way they live and snack, and we need a name that will capture all of the—

[JON*'s hand is up.*]

Yes?

**JON**

How about "Nutrafat"?

**JUDY**

[*Beat.*]

Jon, at this point in time we're really just idea-generating, okay? We're brainstorming, free-associating . . . It's a creative-process-unlocking session. We're not at the naming phase yet. Okay: concepts, people?

**ALL**

[*The band joins in. Slow, then faster.*]

**STEPHEN [KEYBOARD]**

Health.

**MARKET RESEARCH GUY**

Goodness.

**KONRAD [BASS]**

Freedom.

**MATT [GUITAR]**

Dawn.

**STEPHEN**

New Dawn.

**JUDY**

Hello!

[*Beat.*]

Free-Dawn.

**STEPHEN**

[*Aside.*]

She's good.

[*Everyone's looking at* JON.]

**JON**

[*Hesitantly.*]

Hope.

**MARKET RESEARCH GUY**

Hm?

**JON**

Hope.

**MARKET RESEARCH GUY**

Dignity.

**CLAYTON [DRUMS]**

Freedom.

**KONRAD**

I said that already. America.

**MATT**

Destiny.

**STEPHEN**

Manifest Destiny.

**JUDY**

Inalienable rights.

**JON**

The right to be skinny

**MARKET RESEARCH GUY**

[*Angrily, to* JON.]

The bill of rights.

**JON**

[*Cowed.*]

What is your problem?

**CLAYTON**

The Founding Fathers.

**KONRAD**

The Pilgrims.

**MATT**

The first Thanksgiving.

**STEPHEN**

Family.

**JUDY**

Love.

**MARKET RESEARCH GUY**

Sex.

**CLAYTON**

Pleasure.

**KONRAD**

Desire.

**MATT**

Lust.

**STEPHEN**

Urge.

**JUDY**

Hot.

**MARKET RESEARCH GUY**

Touch me.

**CLAYTON**

Yes.

**KONRAD**

There.

**MATT**

Touch me again.

**STEPHEN**

Wow!

**JUDY**

Yummy!

**JON**

Where is this going?

**JUDY**

Okay, terrific! Now I want to move to phase two, turning these general concepts into specific "idea avenues" that will create a context for a process that will facilitate the development of a model that will . . .

[JON *'s hand is up. She sighs.*]

Yes, Jon.

**JON**

I've got it.

**JUDY**

You've got what?

**JON**

I've got the name for the stuff.

**JUDY**

Jon, that's not where we're . . .

[*Gives up.*]

Oh, all right, what is it?

**JON**

"Chubstitute."

[*Beat.*]

Rather than call security, Judy allows me to leave the building under my own power.

# Scene 9

[*The Beemer.* JON *and* MICHAEL. JON *driving.*]

**JON**

So much for my market research career.

**MICHAEL**

Damn it, Jon, I'm gonna hear about this.

**JON**

They told me to be creative. I was creative.

**MICHAEL**

Bullshit. You didn't even try.

**JON**

Hey, I tried.

**MICHAEL**

Chubstitute?

**JON**

Come on. How can you take that stuff seriously?

**MICHAEL**

Because they pay me to. Get over in that lane.

**JON**

What airline are you?

**MICHAEL**

Delta.

**JON**

I see it.

**MICHAEL**

This wasn't a joke, you know. I really had to push for you.

**JON**

I didn't belong there, Mike.

**MICHAEL**

Maybe not. But . . . Jon, for me this is it. It's not some show I can rewrite, or throw away if it's not working. It's real life.

[*Beat.*]

**JON**

Don't you ever miss acting?

**MICHAEL**

I don't miss starving.

**JON**

But you were really good.

**MICHAEL**

Not good enough. Right here is fine.

[*Beat.*]

**JON**

Mike. You all right?

**MICHAEL**

Yeah.

**JON**

You sure? You haven't had more than a couple of days at home for weeks.

**MICHAEL**

They get me the best hotels. I'm not complaining.

**JON**

I know. But you've really been going all-out lately.

**MICHAEL**

I like it. Keeps me distracted.

**JON**

From what?

**MICHAEL**

Nothing.

[*Beat.*]

I just—sometimes I wonder. The life you said Susan wants. It doesn't sound so bad. Some peace, you know? Love. A family . . . If the chance for those things is there, maybe you should grab it.

**JON**

Yeah?

**MICHAEL**

Sometimes I wish I could.

# 7. Real Life

SUNLIGHT
THROUGH THE WINDOW
ACROSS FROM YOUR BED
BEAUTY IS STILL
CAN YOU SEE IT?
WHAT MORE CAN YOU WANT?

IS THIS REAL LIFE?
IS THIS REAL LIFE?

HEARTBEATS
OF YOUR CHILDREN
ASLEEP IN THE NEXT ROOM
TRUST SO STILL
CAN YOU HEAR IT?
WHAT MORE CAN YOU WANT?

| **MICHAEL** | **JON** |
|---|---|
| IS THIS REAL LIFE? | REAL LIFE |
| IS THIS REAL LIFE? | IS THIS REAL, IS THIS |
| | REAL LIFE? |

**MICHAEL**

WHY DO WE SEEK OUT ECSTASY

**MICHAEL and JON**

IN ALL THE WRONG PLACES
WHY IS IT HARD TO SEE
THAT HEAVEN CAN HAVE SIMPLER FACES

**MICHAEL**

WARM BREATH
OF AN ANGEL

**MICHAEL and SUSAN**

AWAKE, NEXT TO YOU
LOVE'S SO STILL
CAN YOU FEEL IT?
WHAT MORE DO YOU WANT?

**MICHAEL**

IS THIS REAL LIFE?
IS THIS REAL LIFE?

IS THIS REAL LIFE?
IS THIS REAL LIFE?

**JON and SUSAN**

REAL LIFE
IS THIS REAL, IS THIS
REAL LIFE?
REAL LIFE
IS THIS REAL, IS THIS
REAL LIFE?

**MICHAEL**

IS THIS REAL LIFE?

I gotta go.

**JON**

Have a safe trip, okay?

**MICHAEL**

I'll see you in a couple of days. Don't wreck the car.

**JON**

Tick . . . tick . . . tick.

# Scene 10

It takes me one and a half hours to get back to Manhattan and park the Beemer. I've got to go straight to a *Superbia* rehearsal. We're just running through the musical numbers in preparation for the workshop.

I need something fast. All that driving. All that talk about fat substitutes. On 9th Avenue I duck into a nondescript storefront. Only one thing can cure me now.

## 8. Sugar

SHE CAN BE WHITE,
SHE CAN BE BROWN.
SHE'S ALWAYS EASY
GOIN' DOWN—GOIN' DOWN

SHE DON'T CARE—WHAT I LOOK LIKE
HOW I DRESS.
NEVER SAYS "NO."
ALWAYS SAYS "YES."

OH—OH—OH, SUGAR, SHE'S REFINED.
FOR A SMALL PRICE SHE BLOWS MY MIND.
SUGAR—SHE'S GOT THE POWER
SOOTHES MY SOUL FOR HALF AN HOUR,
HALF AN HOUR—HALF AN HOUR—HALF AN HOUR

I grew up on Tony the Tiger and Cap'n Crunch, but unlike other Boomer Juniors haven't progressed to more socially accepted fixes, like Ben and Jerry's. I go for the original high-powered numb-busting goodness of the Hostess Twinkie snack cake.

The only problem is, it's humiliating to buy a Twinkie. I walk up to the counter feeling like I'm seventeen and buying condoms for the first time.

**COUNTER GUY [MICHAEL]**

Yeah?

**JON**

Hi, yeah, I'll just take these, uh, double-A batteries, and a pack of the Bic pens, and uh, a Wall Street Journal, and a Mademoiselle . . .

**COUNTER GUY**

And four packages of Twinkies.

**JON**

Right.

**KARESSA [SUSAN]**

Jon?

**JON**

Oh my God.

**KARESSA**

Jon, hi!

**JON**

It's Karessa Johnson! She's in the show. She's incredibly hot. That's not why I cast her; that would be wrong. She is talented and she's got a great voice, but let's face it, I've fantasized about her more than once and now here she is in line behind me and she's buying an Evian water and a package of rice cakes.

**KARESSA**

How's it going?

**JON**

Great! You?

**KARESSA**

Great! I am so excited about the show, it is going to be so good, you are so gifted, I've been telling everyone . . .

**JON**

Really?

**KARESSA**

It has been so great working with you, I just think it's so incredible, you're so young but you're such a mature talent—

**Raúl Esparza**

Jerry Dixon, Amy Spanger, and Raúl Esparza

**Amy Spanger and Raúl Esparza**

Jerry Dixon, left, and Raúl Esparza

**Joey McIntyre, left, who replaced Raúl Esparza, and Jerry Dixon**

Joey McIntyre

Joey McIntyre and Natascia Diaz, who replaced Amy Spanger

Neil Patrick Harris in the 2005 Menier Chocolate Factory production in London

**COUNTER GUY**

You want me to bag these or you want to eat them here?

**JON**

Bag, please.

**KARESSA**

What are those?

**JON**

Nothing. They're snack cakes. They're not unlike rice cakes, only cylindrical and injected with cream.

**KARESSA**

Twinkies! Oh my God. I love them!

**JON**

You do?

**KARESSA**

SHE'S MY HONEY
SHE'S MY TART
I'M HER CREAM PUFF
SHE'S MY SWEETHEART

**JON**

KNOCKS ME OUT,
STRIPS ME BARE,

**ALL**

SUGAR—SUGAR—SUGAR

**JON**

I WON'T CARE.

**COUNTER GUY**

LATE AT NIGHT

**COUNTER GUY and KARESSA**

WHEN I'M SAD AND LONELY

**ALL**

ONE THING ONLY
CURES MY BLUES.

**JON and COUNTER GUY**

STRESSED OUT

**KARESSA**

BURNED OUT

**ALL**

HANGIN' BY A STRING
SUGAR—SUGAR—SUGAR,
I WON'T FEEL A THING
SUGAR SO SWEET

<table>
<tr><th>JON</th><th>KARESSA and<br>COUNTER GUY</th></tr>
<tr><td>ONLY THING I KNOW IS<br>THAT SHE MAKES MY<br>LIFE SUCH A MESS</td><td><br><br>OH YES</td></tr>
<tr><td>SUGAR OH YEAH<br>SUGAR OH YEAH</td><td>SUGAR SUGAR OH YEAH<br>SUGAR SUGAR</td></tr>
</table>

**ALL**

SUGAR, OH YEAH—SUGAR, OH YEAH
S-U-G-A-R

# Scene 11

**JON**

Rehearsal goes well. I think we're going to be ready for the performance on Thursday. I'm so excited I can barely sit still.

Maybe this is it. Maybe I really have written the show that will reinvent musicals for our generation—the *Hair* of the '90s—the cultural lightning rod that will energize the twenty-something generation, we "slackers," raised on The Brady Bunch and Reaganomics, armed with nothing but credit cards, VCRs, and *Interview* magazine, blowing like tumbleweeds through the '90s, fighting off the savage arrows of apathy, illiteracy, innumeracy, exploding Visa bills, eating disorders, sexually transmitted diseases, political correctness . . .

**KARESSA**

Oh my God, that is all so true!

**JON**

Karessa's actually listening to my wired babbling. She walked me home. She's really nice.

When I get upstairs Susan's waiting for me.

**SUSAN**

Who were you walking home with?

**JON**

What?

**SUSAN**

I saw you from the window.

**JON**

She's in Superbia. We were discussing the show.

**SUSAN**

You kissed her.

**JON**

On the cheek. She's in the show! It's a cast thing.

**SUSAN**

Look, I don't care about that. I . . .

**JON**

Susan's holding a Medium Brown Bag. She's packing. I see a sweater, some underwear, her extra contact lens stuff. Her "things."

What's going on?

**SUSAN**

I got a job.

**JON**

That's great!

**SUSAN**

Teaching. Real dancers this time. With a company in Northampton. I'll be gone a couple of weeks.

**JON**

Well, if it's just a couple of weeks . . .

**SUSAN**

Or a month. And . . . it might lead to something else up there.

**JON**

Something else . . . permanently?

**SUSAN**

Maybe. Jon, don't look so surprised. It's not like we're getting anywhere.

**JON**

What do you mean?

**SUSAN**

I can feel us slipping apart.

**JON**

Look, I know you'd like to leave New York. I know you want to make a change. So do I. And after my birthday, after the workshop—

**SUSAN**

I wish everything didn't depend on what happens at the workshop. What if it doesn't go exactly the way you want? What if you turn thirty and nothing's changed? I'm worried you're setting yourself up for a big disappointment.

**JON**

Maybe you're right. Maybe you're right. I don't know . . .

**SUSAN**

I don't want to be disappointed either. It's not—

## 9. See Her Smile

**JON**

IT'S NOT YOU, SHE SAYS
IT'S JUST THAT LIFE'S SO HARD
WE ALL GET BLUE, I SAY
HANG ON TIGHT—I'LL BE YOUR BODYGUARD

SOMETHING'S BREAKING MY BABY'S HEART
SOMETHING'S BREAKING MY BABY'S HEART
SOMETHING'S BREAKING MY BABY'S HEART
OH—I JUST WANT TO SEE HER SMILE

IT'S SUCH A DRAG, SHE SAYS
WHEN THE WORLD'S SO MEAN
IT'S JUST A RED FLAG—I SAY
GOTTA LOOK FOR THE GREEN

OH OH OH
SOMETHING'S BREAKING MY BABY'S HEART
SOMETHING'S BREAKING MY BABY'S HEART
SOMETHING'S BREAKING MY BABY'S HEART

**JON and MICHAEL**

OH

**JON**

I JUST WANT TO SEE HER SMILE

**SUSAN**

I'm not leaving till next week. I'll see you at your party, okay?

**JON**

Hold on. Look, we're both tired. I've been impossible. I'm sorry. I've been hysterical . . .

**SUSAN**

It's not just you. I know I've been demanding . . .

**JON**

Stay here? We don't have to solve everything tonight. We'll order some dinner, go to bed early, just be together. Okay?

**SUSAN**

No. I want to go home.

**JON**

Stay. It's late. It's a long way. Two subways and a bus . . .

**SUSAN**

I'll take a cab.

**JON**

CYNICAL TOWN
CAN BE TOUGH ON AN ANGEL

**JON and MICHAEL**

CLIP HER WINGS, BABY,
ONE TWO THREE

**JON**

I'M HER CLOWN CAUSE

**JON and MICHAEL**

A LAUGHING ANGEL'S
RICHER THAN KINGS,

**JON**

OH, BABY—DON'T YOU SEE?
BABY—DON'T YOU AGREE?

WISH I KNEW WHY, SHE SAYS
BUT ON A SUNNY DAY I FIND THE RAIN

**JON or JON and MICHAEL**

LET'S GIVE IT A TRY, I SAY
WE CAN DANCE RIGHT THROUGH THE PAIN

| **JON** | **MICHAEL and SUSAN** |
|---|---|
| SOMETHING'S BREAKING | OO—IS THIS REAL LIFE? |
| MY BABY'S HEART | |
| SOMETHING'S BREAKING | IS THIS REAL, IS THIS |
| MY BABY'S HEART | |
| SOMETHING'S BREAKING | REAL LIFE? |
| MY BABY'S HEART | |

**ALL**

OH OH OH OH OH

**JON**

I JUST WANT TO SEE HER SMILE

JUST WANT TO SEE HER SMILE
JUST WANT TO SEE HER SMILE
JUST WANT TO SEE HER
JUST WANT TO SEE HER . . .

**SUSAN**

Don't worry about the workshop. I know it will be wonderful.

**JON**

Hey, Susan, don't go. Look, I'm sorry—

. . . SMILE.

She's gone.

# Scene 12

**JON**

The workshop. The show's about to start. The room is totally empty. The show's about to start and I'm staring at sixty empty folding chairs. No one's here. NO ONE HAS FUCKING SHOWED UP! Not Susan, not Michael, not even Rosa fucking Stevens!

**KARESSA**

Jon.

**JON**

Karessa! Hey!

**KARESSA**

Hey, boy genius.

**JON**

Where the fuck is everyone?

**KARESSA**

We don't start for over an hour, Jon. The house isn't open yet. Relax.

**JON**

She kisses me.

**KARESSA**

It's going to be great.

**JON**

The next fifty-five minutes are a blur. Michael comes in first.

**MICHAEL**

Hey, buddy.

**JON**

Mike! Thank God.

**MICHAEL**

Where should I sit?

**JON**

Anywhere. Thank you so much for coming.

**MICHAEL**

Are you kidding? Wild horses, Jon.

**JON**

There's an elegant older lady with a cigarette holder.
She looks familiar.

**ROSA**

Hello, darling.

**JON**

Rosa Stevens! It's been so long since I've actually had personal contact with my agent I didn't recognize her.

**ROSA**

It's going to go marvelously, don't you worry.

**JON**

To my surprise, she hugs me.

**ROSA**

You're perspiring a bit heavily, dear. Before they start you might want to go and towel off.

**JON**

She glides away, I wipe my face . . .

**DAD**

HEL-lo.

**JON**

Hi, Dad.

**DAD**

Pretty good crowd.

**JON**

Not bad, right?

**DAD**

Are they paying?

**JON**

Not technically, no.

**DAD**

Next time. I'm proud of you. Write if you get work.

**JON**

Hang by your thumbs.

Suddenly the room is full of friends and the interesting people Rosa promised, and the band is tuning up, and just before the lights go down there is a stir and a latecomer darts for his seat—Is it? It's—YES! IT'S HIM!! He's HERE!! My guru of the musical theatre, the most interesting person of all. Ste—— Sond——.

**JON**

And my fear . . . my fear gathers itself into a ball in my stomach and rises, pulsing, into my throat; it moves on into my skull, where it takes up residence, hissing and shuddering . . . and then, miraculously, it keeps going: floating up, higher, out of my head entirely, dissolving into the air as it leaves my body—and what remains behind is pure excitement and hope.

Hi, I'm Jon. Thanks for coming. Today you're gonna see a new musical called *Superbia* . . . written by me. . . . Thank you . . . I don't really have anything to say except thanks for coming, and I already said that . . . so now I'd better just get the hell off so these people can do their work. Enjoy the show . . .

[*The band plays part of the* Superbia *overture.*]

And after that it's a blur again . . .
At least until Karessa begins her solo.

## 10. Come to Your Senses

**KARESSA**

YOU'RE ON THE AIR
I'M UNDERGROUND
SIGNAL'S FADING
CAN'T BE FOUND
I FINALLY OPEN UP
FOR YOU I WOULD DO ANYTHING
BUT YOU'VE TURNED OFF THE VOLUME
JUST WHEN I'VE BEGUN TO SING

COME TO YOUR SENSES
DEFENSES ARE NOT THE WAY TO GO
AND YOU KNOW
OR AT LEAST YOU KNEW

EVERYTHING'S STRANGE,
YOU'VE CHANGED AND I DON'T KNOW WHAT TO DO
TO GET THROUGH
I DON'T KNOW WHAT TO DO

I HAVE TO LAUGH
WE SURE PUT ON A SHOW
LOVE IS PASSÉ IN THIS DAY AND AGE
HOW CAN WE EXPECT IT TO GROW?

YOU AS THE KNIGHT
ME AS THE QUEEN
ALL I'VE GOT TONIGHT
IS STATIC ON A SCREEN

COME TO YOUR SENSES
THE FENCES INSIDE ARE NOT FOR REAL
IF WE FEEL AS WE DID AND I DO

CAN'T YOU RECALL
WHEN THIS ALL BEGAN
IT WAS ONLY YOU AND ME
IT WAS ONLY ME AND YOU

BUT NOW THE AIR IS FILLED WITH CONFUSION
WE'VE REPLACED CARE WITH ILLUSION

IT'S COOL TO BE COLD
NOTHING LASTS ANYMORE
LOVE BECOMES DISPOSABLE
THIS IS THE SHAPE OF THINGS
WE CANNOT IGNORE

COME TO YOUR SENSES
SUSPENSE IS FINE
IF YOU'RE JUST AN EMPTY IMAGE
EMANATING OUT OF A SCREEN

BABY, BE REAL,
YOU CAN FEEL AGAIN
YOU DON'T NEED A MUSIC BOX MELODY
TO KNOW WHAT I MEAN

DEEP IN MY EYES
WHAT DO YOU SEE?
DEEP IN MY SIGHS
LISTEN TO ME

LET THE MUSIC COMMENCE FROM INSIDE
NOT ONLY ONE SENSE, BUT USE ALL FIVE

COME TO YOUR SENSES
COME TO YOUR SENSES
COME TO YOUR SENSES
BABY, COME BACK ALIVE

# Scene 13

**ROSA [MICHAEL]**

Jon? It's Rosa calling. I just wanted to say congratulations.

**JON**

Rosa! Thank you so much for calling.

**ROSA**

Well, you left eleven messages this morning, dear.

**JON**

Oh, right.

**ROSA**

I think you should be very proud. Everything went beautifully.

**JON**

Really? Thanks! The cast was good, I think, and the audience seemed into it—did you see Ste—— Sond——?

**ROSA**

Stevie? Oh yes, I wanted to chat but he must have snuck out early. But everyone had fun. Congratulations, honey. We'll talk soon.

**JON**

Rosa, uh, wait—Do you think . . . what do you think will happen? I mean, does anyone want to move it to the next step, or . . . I mean, the interesting people, did anybody say anything?

**ROSA**

Well, Jon, I think everyone was just so intrigued by your talent, and they can't wait to see what happens next.

**JON**

What happens next.

**ROSA**

Yes, be sure to keep me up to date on what you're working on.

**JON**

Nothing? No nibbles? Nothing?

**ROSA**

Honey, we always knew it's a little quirky for Broadway, and the cast is awfully big for Off-, and the futuristic thing means sets are expensive, and musical theatre is Newark Airport and you're snowed in at Buffalo—and now, having plucked out your heart and eaten it like a piece of ripe fruit, I'll leave you to sweep up the fragments of your shattered dreams, bye-bye, honey! Happy birthday!

**JON**

I get three other calls from friends in the business and they're all like that.

# Scene 14

**MICHAEL**

Jon?

**JON**

I go to Michael's office.

[*Beat.*]

I can't do this, Mike.

**MICHAEL**

Uh?

**JON**

The theatre, the music. I gave it my shot. I think I've given it an honest try, with all the talent and effort I've got. And it hasn't worked. I'm not sorry I tried. I'm proud of it, but now it's time to take a hard look at my situation and not be egotistical, not delude myself, just admit it's time to move on. I've been stuck. Everyone else, you and Susan, have kept moving. I'm the only one still here banging my head against the wall. My head hurts. I'm going to stop for a while. The thing is, I can always come back to it, if I want, when I'm older, when I'm smarter, when I've figured out a little more clearly what it is I want to do.

[*Beat.*]

I feel better. Just hearing myself say it, I already feel better.

[*Beat.*]

**MICHAEL**

You're right. I think your heart is telling you something, and I think what you're saying takes courage. I think it takes courage to let all that stuff go. I'm proud of you.

**JON**

You are?

**MICHAEL**

No, of course not, you fucking idiot. What is the matter with you?

**JON**

I can't keep doing this! The show—

**MICHAEL**

Listen, Jon, the show was very good. You should be proud of it. Everyone loved it.

**JON**

My friends loved it.

**MICHAEL**

What's wrong with that?

**JON**

No one wants to produce it.

**MICHAEL**

It's a workshop. You'll keep working, keep developing it. Or you'll start something else.

**JON**

Spend another five years on a show that doesn't go anywhere? I swear to God I'll explode. By then I'll be thirty-five—

**MICHAEL**

Thirty-five, thirty, who cares? It's meaningless! Focus on something important! Do your work!

**JON**

That's easy for you to say! You've got a job, an apartment, a fucking BMW.

**MICHAEL**

Hold on. We both made choices.

**JON**

I don't want to sell out.

**MICHAEL**

You mean like me.

**JON**

You said it, I didn't.

**MICHAEL**

If it's the car and apartment that's bothering you, I'm sorry. Why shouldn't I enjoy those things while I have the chance?

**JON**

That's not what I'm—

**MICHAEL**

Jon. Listen to me. All of this—this is just your fear talking. You have to take control of it. You have to thank your brain for sharing that fear, then ignore it and go on. Fear is like Newark Airport—

**JON**

SCREW NEWARK AIRPORT! WHAT THE HELL DO YOU KNOW ABOUT FEAR? WHAT DO YOU KNOW ABOUT ANYTHING?

**MICHAEL**

I know I'm sick, Jon, and I'm not going to get any better.

[*Beat.*]

**JON**

When did you . . . How long have . . . ?

**MICHAEL**

Two weeks. I wanted to tell you earlier, but I couldn't.

[*Beat.*]

Look, if you don't mind, it's the middle of the day, and I have a lot of work to do. Close the door when you go, okay?

# Scene 15

**JON**

In the elevator I think of sleepaway camp. How Michael bribed Jim Shanahan with M&M's to switch bunks so we could whisper in the night.

I remember being teenagers, when our families rented houses in Hyannis and we'd walk down the beach, hop the fence, and swim for hours together up and down the shore.

I think of our first summer back from college, when we reunited for a joint on the Kennedy breakwater, and Mike told me he was gay.

The sun is fighting off the January clouds as it sinks behind the park. I run from 53rd and Fifth to East Drive, past the Zoo, the Dairy. A pay phone! I jam in a quarter, dial Mike—his machine picks up—I try again—same thing—goddamn it!—slam the phone down and keep running. I'm running. Past the skaters, past the Carousel, the statue of Shakespeare.

The Sheep's Meadow is empty. I hop the fence and run to the middle of the field. Rain begins falling and I spin myself in circles and stagger around like a wino.

The TICK-BOOM, TICK-BOOM is so loud I can't hear the rain on the grass. I can't hear the wind.

I'm about to scream when I realize I'm not alone. Watching me from the hill in front of me are hundreds of seagulls. I sprint right into them, waving my arms like a castaway on a desert island spotting a rescue plane.

They fly up into the air en masse, only to land across the meadow, on another hill. I talk to them. MY FRIEND IS DYING. I'M LOST. I'M AFRAID. I run past the fountain, the waterfall, up through the woods, to the top of the Belvedere Castle. I look down into the empty Delacorte Theatre. I see an old rehearsal piano, sitting out under a tarp, below the trees. I climb down, hop another fence, and pull off the tarp.

## 11. Why

WHEN I WAS NINE
MICHAEL AND I
ENTERED A TALENT SHOW
DOWN AT THE Y

NINE A.M., WENT TO REHEARSE
BY SOME STAIRS
MIKE COULDN'T SING
BUT I SAID, "NO ONE CARES"

WE SANG "YELLOW BIRD"
AND "LET'S GO FLY A KITE"

OVER AND OVER AND OVER
TILL WE GOT IT RIGHT

WHEN WE EMERGED
FROM THE YMCA
THREE O'CLOCK SUN
HAD MADE THE GRASS HAY

I THOUGHT
HEY—WHAT A WAY TO SPEND THE DAY
HEY—WHAT A WAY TO SPEND THE DAY
I MAKE A VOW—RIGHT HERE AND NOW
I'M GONNA SPEND MY TIME THIS WAY

WHEN I WAS SIXTEEN
MICHAEL AND I
GOT PARTS IN *WEST SIDE*
AT WHITE PLAINS HIGH

THREE O'CLOCK, WENT TO REHEARSE
IN THE GYM
MIKE PLAYED "DOC"—WHO DIDN'T SING—
FINE WITH HIM

WE SANG "GOT A ROCKET IN YOUR POCKET"
AND "THE JETS ARE GONNA HAVE THEIR DAY—TONIGHT"
OVER AND OVER AND OVER
TILL WE GOT IT RIGHT

WHEN WE EMERGED—
WIPED OUT BY THE PLAY
NINE O'CLOCK STARS
AND MOON LIT THE WAY

I THOUGHT
HEY—WHAT A WAY TO SPEND THE DAY
HEY—WHAT A WAY TO SPEND THE DAY
I MADE A VOW—I WONDER NOW
AM I CUT OUT TO SPEND MY TIME THIS WAY?

WITH ONLY SO MUCH TIME TO SPEND
DON'T WANT TO WASTE THE TIME I'M GIVEN
"HAVE IT ALL—PLAY THE GAME" SOME RECOMMEND
I'M AFRAID IT JUST MAY BE TIME TO GIVE IN

I'M TWENTY-NINE
MICHAEL AND I
LIVE ON THE WEST SIDE
OF SOHO, N.Y.

NINE A.M.,
I WRITE A LYRIC OR TWO
MIKE SINGS HIS SONG
NOW ON MAD AVENUE

I SING, "COME TO YOUR SENSES
DEFENSES ARE NOT THE WAY TO GO"
OVER AND OVER AND OVER
TILL I GET IT RIGHT
WHEN I EMERGE
FROM B MINOR OR A
FIVE O'CLOCK—DINER CALLS,
"I'M ON MY WAY"

I THINK
HEY—WHAT A WAY TO SPEND THE DAY
HEY—WHAT A WAY TO SPEND THE DAY
I MAKE A VOW—RIGHT HERE AND NOW
I'M GONNA SPEND MY TIME THIS WAY
I'M GONNA SPEND MY TIME THIS WAY

# Scene 16

Saturday night. It's my thirtieth birthday. Thirty. Three-O. Hey, it's no big deal. Just three decades. What's thirty?

## 12. 30/90 (Reprise)

DON'T FREAK OUT—DON'T STRIKE OUT
CAN'T FIGHT IT—LIKE CITY HALL
AT LEAST YOU'RE NOT ALONE
YOUR FRIENDS ARE THERE TOO—

The apartment is warm and noisy. I realize I don't want to escape to the roof, or fly to Cuba, or hide in the bathroom. I grab a beer and wade into the crowd.

INTO MY HANDS NOW—THE BALL IS PASSED
I WANT THE SPOILS—BUT NOT TOO FAST
THE WORLD IS CALLING—IT'S NOW OR NEVERLAND

THIRTY NINETY THIRTY NINETY
THIRTY NINETY THIRTY NINETY . . .

I open gifts. Mostly gag stuff. Three Gumbys, two Silly Puttys, and a TV Themes CD. Susan's here. I don't know what to say. She doesn't either.

When are you leaving?

**SUSAN**

Tomorrow.

**JON**

I'll really miss you.

**SUSAN**

I'll miss you too.

**JON**

Will you write?

**SUSAN**

I will if you will.

**JON**

She hands me a large book. I open it. Blank music manuscript paper. A thousand sheets.

Thank you.

**SUSAN**

Happy birthday, Jon. Don't forget to breathe.

**JON**

She disappears into the crowd and suddenly Michael's beside me. He tosses me a box. I open it. Three belts.

Gucci?

**MICHAEL**

Not Gucci. You're not a Gucci guy. But it's life-affirming to own multiple accessories, and I want you experience that.

**JON**

Thanks, Mike.

**MICHAEL**

Sure thing. Happy birthday, buddy.

**JON**

I'm sorry about yesterday. I wish I had known. I don't know what to say. I'll be there. I promise.

**MICHAEL**

I know you will.

[*Phone ring.*]

**JON**

I let the machine pick up.

**SONDHEIM (V.O.)**

[*Beep.*]

Jon? Steve Sondheim. Rosa gave me your number. Sorry we couldn't talk after the show, I had to rush out. Just wanted to say terrific work. Really. I'd love to get together and talk about it. Give me a call—and congratulations. You're going to have a great future.

[*Beep.*]

**JON**

What do you know?

The dreaded moment arrives. I'm escorted by a gaggle of smiling faces into the next room. People whisper. The lights are turned off.

The darkness is pierced by a blinding glow.

[HE *blows out the candles on the cake.*]

They lead me over to the piano to play.

The tick-tick-booms are softer now. I can barely hear them, and I think if I play loud enough, I can drown them out completely.

## 13. Louder Than Words

WHY DO WE PLAY WITH FIRE?
WHY DO WE RUN OUR FINGER THROUGH THE FLAME?
WHY DO WE LEAVE OUR HAND ON THE STOVE—
ALTHOUGH WE KNOW WE'RE IN FOR SOME PAIN?

OH, WHY DO WE REFUSE TO HANG A LIGHT
WHEN THE STREETS ARE DANGEROUS?
WHY DOES IT TAKE AN ACCIDENT
BEFORE THE TRUTH GETS THROUGH TO US?

CAGES OR WINGS?
WHICH DO YOU PREFER?
ASK THE BIRDS

FEAR OR LOVE, BABY?
DON'T SAY THE ANSWER
ACTIONS SPEAK LOUDER THAN WORDS

**MICHAEL**

WHY SHOULD WE TRY TO BE OUR BEST
WHEN WE CAN JUST GET BY AND STILL GAIN?
WHY DO WE NOD OUR HEADS

**MICHAEL and JON**

ALTHOUGH WE KNOW

**MICHAEL**

THE BOSS IS WRONG AS RAIN?

**JON**

WHY SHOULD WE BLAZE A TRAIL
WHEN THE WELL-WORN PATH SEEMS SAFE AND

**JON and SUSAN**

SO INVITING?

**SUSAN**

HOW—AS WE TRAVEL CAN WE

**SUSAN and JON**

SEE THE DISMAY—
AND KEEP FROM FIGHTING?

| **JON** | **MICHAEL and SUSAN** |
|---|---|
| CAGES OR WINGS? | CAGES OR WINGS |
| WHICH DO YOU PREFER? | |
| ASK THE BIRDS | AH . . . |

**ALL**

FEAR OR LOVE, BABY?
DON'T SAY THE ANSWER

**JON**

ACTIONS SPEAK LOUDER
THAN WORDS

**MICHAEL and SUSAN**

LOUDER THAN, LOUDER THAN

**JON**

WHAT DOES IT TAKE—
TO WAKE UP A GENERATION?

**ALL**

HOW CAN YOU MAKE SOMEONE
TAKE OFF AND FLY?

**JON**

IF WE DON'T WAKE UP
AND SHAKE UP THE NATION
WE'LL EAT THE DUST OF
THE WORLD,
WONDERING WHY

**MICHAEL and SUSAN**

WHY

**SUSAN**

WHY DO WE STAY WITH LOVERS

**SUSAN and JON**

WHO WE KNOW, DOWN DEEP

**SUSAN**

JUST AREN'T RIGHT?

**JON**

WHY WOULD WE RATHER

**ALL**

PUT OURSELVES THROUGH HELL
THAN SLEEP ALONE AT NIGHT?

**JON**

WHY DO WE FOLLOW LEADERS WHO NEVER LEAD?

**MICHAEL**

WHY DOES IT TAKE CATASTROPHE TO START A REVOLUTION

**MICHAEL and SUSAN**

IF WE'RE SO FREE, TELL ME WHY?

**JON**

SOMEONE TELL ME WHY
SO MANY PEOPLE BLEED?

**JON**

CAGES OR WINGS?
WHICH DO YOU PREFER?
ASK THE BIRDS

**MICHAEL and SUSAN**

CAGES OR WINGS

AH . . .

**ALL**

FEAR OR LOVE, BABY?
DON'T SAY THE ANSWER

**JON**

ACTIONS SPEAK LOUDER
THAN

**MICHAEL and SUSAN**

LOUDER THAN, LOUDER THAN

LOUDER THAN, LOUDER THAN

**ALL**

[*A cappella.*]

CAGES OR WINGS?
WHICH DO YOU PREFER?

**JON**

ASK THE BIRDS

**MICHAEL and SUSAN**

AH . . .

**ALL**

FEAR OR LOVE, BABY?
DON'T SAY THE ANSWER

**JON**

ACTIONS SPEAK LOUDER
THAN
THEY SPEAK LOUDER
ACTIONS SPEAK LOUDER
THAN . . .

**MICHAEL and SUSAN**

LOUDER THAN, LOUDER
THAN, OOH
LOUDER THAN, LOUDER THAN
WORDS

[*The music turns into "Happy Birthday."*]

## Biographies

**Jonathan Larson** (book, music, and lyrics) received the 1996 Pulitzer Prize for Drama for *Rent*. He also won the 1996 Tony Award for Best Musical and the 1994 Richard Rodgers Award for *Rent* and twice received The Gilman and Gonzalez-Falla Theatre Foundation's Commendation Award. In 1988, he won the Richard Rodgers Development Grant for his rock musical *Superbia*, which was staged at Playwrights Horizons. In 1989, he was granted the Stephen Sondheim Award from the American Music Theatre Festival, where he contributed to the musical *Sitting on the Edge of the Future*. He composed the score for the musical *J.P. Morgan Saves the Nation*, which was presented by En Garde Arts in 1995. Mr. Larson performed his rock monologue *tick, tick . . . BOOM!* at Second Stage Theatre, the Village Gate, and New York Theatre Workshop. In addition to scoring and songwriting for *Sesame Street*, he created music for a number of children's book-cassettes, including Steven Spielberg's *An American Tail* and *The Land Before Time*. Other film scores include work for *Rolling Stone* magazine publisher Jann Wenner. He conceived, directed, and wrote four original songs for *Away We Go!*, a musical video for children. *Rent*, his rock opera based on *La Bohème*, had its world premiere on February 13, 1996, at New York Theatre Workshop. Mr. Larson died unexpectedly of an aortic aneurysm on January 25, 1996, ten days before his thirty-sixth birthday.

**Robyn Goodman** (Introduction) produced two Tony Award–winning musicals, *Avenue Q* (2004) and *In the Heights* (2008). Other Broadway credits include *Metamorphoses* (Drama Desk Award), *A Class Act*, *Steel Magnolias*, *Barefoot in the Park*, *High Fidelity*, and *West Side Story* (2009). Off-Broadway she produced *Bat Boy*; *tick, tick . . . Boom!*; *Our Lady of 121st Street*; *Red Light Winter*; and the award-winning *Altar Boyz*. She was co-founder and artistic director of the Second Stage Theatre for thirteen years and supervising producer of ABC's *One Life to Live* for four years. Besides running her own production company, Aged in Wood, LLC, she is currently the artistic consultant to the Roundabout Theatre Company where she curates their Underground series.

CPSIA information can be obtained
at www.ICGtesting.com
Printed in the USA
LVHW050337190122
708648LV00014B/1029

9 781557 837448